MW01127167

Mysteries of the Rosary

Children's Coloring Book

Susan A. Howard

Praised be Jesus Christ, now and forever!

Copyright ©2017 by Susan A. Howard and Total180 Press.

All rights reserved. No part of this publication may be reproduced, distributed, or transmitted in any form or by any means, including photocopying, recording, or other electronic or mechanical methods, without the prior written permission of the publisher, except in the case of brief quotations embodied in critical reviews and certain other noncommercial uses permitted by copyright law. For permission requests, write to the publisher, addressed "Attention: Permissions," at the address below.

Total180 Press
18578 Rainier View Rd. SE
Monroe, WA 98272

ISBN# 978-0974411842

Scripture quotations from the New Revised Standard Version Catholic Edition Bible.

What is the Rosary?

The Rosary is a method of praying given to us and and encouraged by Our Lady, the Blessed Virgin Mary, that helps us concentrate on and follow the life and example of Our Lord, Jesus. Through it, we honor God and his Mother, prepare ourselves to receive God's grace, ask God for his help and guidance and ask Mary for her intercession. That's a lot of good!

Each of the Mysteries focuses on different events in the life of Christ that we learn about in Scripture and from the Church's Holy Tradition. The Joyful Mysteries cover events from Jesus' childhood. The Luminous Mysteries cover Jesus' ministry. We remember the Lord's Passion and Death in the Sorrowful Mysteries, and The Glorious Mysteries recall the birth of His Church. Each set of Mysteries recalls five events. For each mystery, we have included a Scripture reference and the fruit - the goodness that grows in us as we continue to pray the rosary - is found in the title banner of each coloring page.

The prayer begins at the crucifix with the sign of the cross and the Apostles' Creed. It is then followed by an Our Father at the first single bead. At each bead in the group of three we say a Hail Mary, one for faith, one for hope and one for love. Then we end the beginning section with a Glory Be. At the next single bead we announce the first mystery and pray the Our Father, followed by a Hail Mary on each of the following ten beads. We end the decade with a Glory Be and the Fatima prayer. Then, we announce the second mystery, and continue the pattern through all five mysteries of the set you have chosen to pray. The universal Church prays a particular set on a particular day, so by following that schedule you can pray in union with Her!

After all the mysteries have been prayed, and you arrive at the Marian medal that connects the decades, say the Hail Holy Queen, and the closing prayer. All of these prayers can be found on the next page and the last page of this book..

Let's begin...Think of some things you'd like to pray for.
(We call them "intentions")

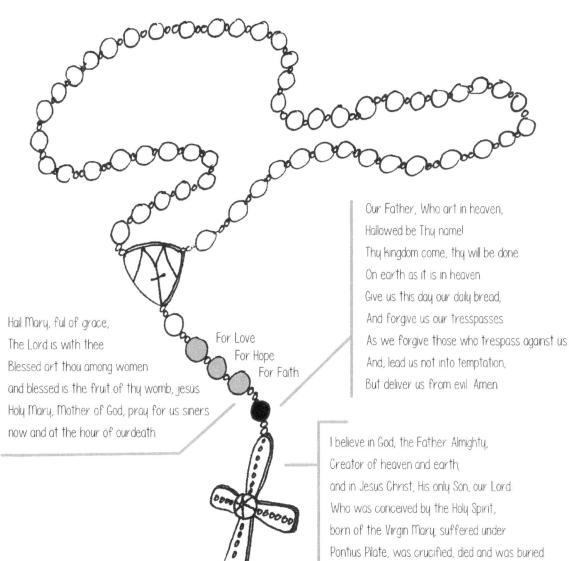

Our Father, Who art in heaven,
Hallowed be Thy name!
Thy kingdom come, thy will be done
On earth as it is in heaven
Give us this day our daily bread,
And forgive us our tresspasses
As we forgive those who trespass against us.
And, lead us not into temptation,
But deliver us from evil. Amen.

Hail Mary, full of grace,
The Lord is with thee
Blessed art thou among women
and blessed is the fruit of thy womb, jesus
Holy Mary, Mother of God, pray for us siners
now and at the hour of ourdeath

For Love
For Hope
For Faith

I believe in God, the Father Almighty,
Creator of heaven and earth;
and in Jesus Christ, His only Son, our Lord.
Who was conceived by the Holy Spirit,
born of the Virgin Mary, suffered under
Pontius Pilate, was crucified, died and was buried.
He descended into hell; the third day He rose again
from the dead, He ascended into heaven,
and is seated at the right hand of God the Father Almighty,
thence He shall come to judge the living and the dead.
I believe in the Holy Spirit, the Holy Catholic Church,
the communion of Saints, the forgiveness of sins,
the resurrection of the body, and life everlasting. Amen.

The Joyful Mysteries: Prayed Mondays and Saturdays

The Annunciation
The Birth of Jesus Foretold (Luke 1:26-38)*

In the sixth month the angel Gabriel was sent by God to a town in Galilee called Nazareth, to a virgin engaged to a man whose name was Joseph, of the house of David. The virgin's name was Mary. And he came to her and said, "Greetings, favored one! The Lord is with you." But she was much perplexed by his words and pondered what sort of greeting this might be. The angel said to her, "Do not be afraid, Mary, for you have found favor with God. And now, you will conceive in your womb and bear a son, and you will name him Jesus. He will be great, and will be called the Son of the Most High, and the Lord God will give to him the throne of his ancestor David. He will reign over the house of Jacob forever, and of his kingdom there will be no end." Mary said to the angel, "How can this be, since I am a virgin?" The angel said to her, "The Holy Spirit will come upon you, and the power of the Most High will overshadow you; therefore the child to be born will be holy; he will be called Son of God. And now, your relative Elizabeth in her old age has also conceived a son; and this is the sixth month for her who was said to be barren. For nothing will be impossible with God." Then Mary said, "Here am I, the servant of the Lord; let it be with me according to your word." Then the angel departed from her.

*NRSVCE

The First Joyful Mystery

The Annunciation
Fruit: Humility

The Joyful Mysteries: Prayed Mondays and Saturdays

The Visitation
Mary Visits Elizabeth (Luke 1:39-45)*

In those days Mary set out and went with haste to a
Judean town in the hill country, where she entered
the house of Zechariah and greeted Elizabeth. When
Elizabeth heard Mary's greeting, the child leaped in
her womb. And Elizabeth was filled with the Holy
Spirit and exclaimed with a loud cry, "Blessed are you
among women, and blessed is the fruit of your womb.
And why has this happened to me, that the mother
of my Lord comes to me? For as soon as I heard the
sound of your greeting, the child in my womb leaped
for joy. And blessed is she who believed that there
would be a fulfillment of what was spoken to her by
the Lord."

*NRSVCE

The Second Joyful Mystery

The Visitation
Fruit: Love of Neighbor

The Joyful Mysteries: Prayed Mondays and Saturdays

The Nativity
The Birth of Jesus (Luke 2:1-7)*

In those days a decree went out from Emperor Augustus that all the world should be registered. 2 This was the first registration and was taken while Quirinius was governor of Syria. 3 All went to their own towns to be registered. 4 Joseph also went from the town of Nazareth in Galilee to Judea, to the city of David called Bethlehem, because he was descended from the house and family of David. 5 He went to be registered with Mary, to whom he was engaged and who was expecting a child. 6 While they were there, the time came for her to deliver her child. 7 And she gave birth to her firstborn son and wrapped him in bands of cloth, and laid him in a manger, because there was no place for them in the inn.

*NRSVCE

The Third Joyful Mystery

The Nativity
Fruit: Poverty of Spirit

The Joyful Mysteries: Prayed Mondays and Saturdays

The Presentation
The Birth of Jesus (Luke 2:22-33)*

When the time came for their purification according to the law of Moses, they brought him up to Jerusalem to present him to the Lord (as it is written in the law of the Lord, "Every firstborn male shall be designated as holy to the Lord"), and they offered a sacrifice according to what is stated in the law of the Lord, "a pair of turtledoves or two young pigeons."

Now there was a man in Jerusalem whose name was Simeon; this man was righteous and devout, looking forward to the consolation of Israel, and the Holy Spirit rested on him. It had been revealed to him by the Holy Spirit that he would not see death before he had seen the Lord's Messiah. Guided by the Spirit, Simeon came into the temple, and when the parents brought in the child Jesus, to do for him what was customary under the law, Simeon took him in his arms and praised God, saying,

"Master, now you are dismissing your servant in peace,
according to your word;
for my eyes have seen your salvation,
which you have prepared in the presence of all peoples,
a light for revelation to the Gentiles
and for glory to your people Israel"

And the child's father and mother were amazed at what was being said about him.

*NRSVCE

Presentation of Jesus
Fruit: Obedience to the Law of God

The Joyful Mysteries: Prayed Mondays and Saturdays

Finding Jesus in the Temple
(Luke 2:41-52)*

Now every year his (Jesus's) parents went to Jerusalem for the festival of the Passover. And when he was twelve years old, they went up as usual for the festival. When the festival was ended and they started to return, the boy Jesus stayed behind in Jerusalem, but his parents did not know it. Assuming that he was in the group of travelers, they went a day's journey. Then they started to look for him among their relatives and friends. When they did not find him, they returned to Jerusalem to search for him. After three days they found him in the temple, sitting among the teachers, listening to them and asking them questions. And all who heard him were amazed at his understanding and his answers. When his parents saw him they were astonished; and his mother said to him, "Child, why have you treated us like this? Look, your father and I have been searching for you in great anxiety." He said to them, "Why were you searching for me? Did you not know that I must be in my Father's house?" But they did not understand what he said to them.

Then, he went down with them and came to Nazareth, and was obedient to them. His mother treasured all these things in her heart. And Jesus increased in wisdom and in years, and in divine and human favor.

*NRSVCE

Finding Jesus in the Temple
Fruit: Joy in Finding Jesus in Your Life

Luminous

The Luminous Mysteries: Prayed Thursdays

The Baptism of Jesus
John Baptizes Jesus (Matthew 3: 13-17)*

13Then Jesus came from Galilee to John at the Jordan, to be baptized by him. John would have prevented him, saying, "I need to be baptized by you, and do you come to me?" But Jesus answered him, "Let it be so now, for it is proper for us in this way to fulfill all righteousness." Then he consented. And when Jesus had been baptized, just as he came up from the water, suddenly the heavens were opened to him and he saw the Spirit of God descending like a dove and alighting on him. And a voice from heaven said, "This is my Son, the Beloved, with whom I am well pleased."

*NRSVCE

The First Luminous Mystery

The Baptism of Jesus
Gift: Openness to the Holy Spirit

The Luminous Mysteries: Prayed Thursdays

The Wedding at Cana
Jesus Turns Water to Wine (John 2: 1-11)*

On the third day there was a wedding in Cana of Galilee, and the mother of Jesus was there. Jesus and his disciples had also been invited to the wedding. When the wine gave out, the mother of Jesus said to him, "They have no wine." And Jesus said to her, "Woman, what concern is that to you and to me? My hour has not yet come." His mother said to the servants, "Do whatever he tells you." Now standing there were six stone water jars for the Jewish rites of purification, each holding twenty or thirty gallons. Jesus said to them, "Fill the jars with water." And they filled them up to the brim. He said to them, "Now draw some out, and take it to the chief steward." So they took it. When the steward tasted the water that had become wine, and did not know where it came from (though the servants who had drawn the water knew), the steward called the bridegroom and said to him, "Everyone serves the good wine first, and then the inferior wine after the guests have become drunk. But you have kept the good wine until now." Jesus did this, the first of his signs, in Cana of Galilee, and revealed his glory; and his disciples believed in him.

*NRSVCE

The Second Luminous Mystery

The Wedding of Cana
Fruit: To Jesus Through Mary

The Luminous Mysteries: Prayed Thursdays

The Proclamation of the Kingdom
(Matthew 5: 1-12)*

When Jesus saw the crowds, he went up the mountain, and after he sat down, his disciples came to him. Then he began to speak, and taught them, saying:

"Blessed are the poor in spirit, for theirs is the kingdom of heaven.
"Blessed are those who mourn, for they will be comforted.
"Blessed are the meek, for they will inherit the earth.
"Blessed are those who hunger and thirst for righteousness, for they will be filled.
"Blessed are the merciful, for they will receive mercy.
"Blessed are the pure in heart, for they will see God.
"Blessed are the peacemakers, for they will be called children of God
"Blessed are those who are persecuted for righteousness' sake, for theirs is the kingdom of heaven.
"Blessed are you when people revile you and persecute you and utter all kinds of evil against you falsely on my account.

Rejoice and be glad, for your reward is great in heaven, for in the same way they persecuted the prophets who were before you.

*NRSVCE

The Third Luminous Mystery

Proclaiming the Kingdom
Fruit: Repentence and Trust in God

The Luminous Mysteries: Prayed Thursdays

The Transfiguration
(Mark 9: 2-8)*

Six days later, Jesus took with him Peter and James and John, and led them up a high mountain apart, by themselves And he was transfigured before them, and his clothes became dazzling white, such as no one on earth could bleach them. And there appeared to them Elijah with Moses, who were talking with Jesus. Then Peter said to Jesus, "Rabbi, it is good for us to be here; let us make three dwellings, one for you, one for Moses, and one for Elijah." He did not know what to say, for they were terrified. Then a cloud overshadowed them, and from the cloud there came a voice, "This is my Son, the Beloved; listen to him!" Suddenly when they looked around, they saw no one with them any more, but only Jesus.

*NRSVCE

The Fourth Luminous Mystery

The Transfiguration
Fruit: Desire for Holiness

The Luminous Mysteries: Prayed Thursdays

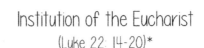

Institution of the Eucharist
(Luke 22: 14-20)*

When the hour came, he took his place at the table, and the apostles
with him. He said to them, "I have eagerly desired to eat this Passover
with you before I suffer; 16 for I tell you, I will not eat it until it is
fulfilled in the kingdom of God." Then he took a cup, and after giving
thanks he said, "Take this and divide it among yourselves; for I tell you
that from now on I will not drink of the fruit of the vine until the
kingdom of God comes." Then he took a loaf of bread, and when he
had given thanks, he broke it and gave it to them, saying, "This is my
body, which is given for you. Do this in remembrance of me." And he
did the same with the cup after supper, saying, "This cup that is
poured out for you is the new covenant in my blood.

*NRSVCE

The Fifth Luminous Mystery

The Institution of the Eucharist
Fruit: Adoration

The Sorrowful Mysteries: Prayed Tuesdays and Fridays

The Agony in the Garden
Jesus Prays in Gethsemane (Matthew 26: 26-46)*

Then Jesus went with them to a place called Gethsemane, and he said to his disciples, "Sit here while I go over there and pray." He took with him Peter and the two sons of Zebedee, and began to be grieved and agitated. Then he said to them, "I am deeply grieved, even to death; remain here, and stay awake with me." And going a little farther, he threw himself on the ground and prayed, "My Father, if it is possible, let this cup pass from me; yet not what I want but what you want." Then he came to the disciples and found them sleeping; and he said to Peter, "So, could you not stay awake with me one hour? Stay awake and pray that you may not come into the time of trial; the spirit indeed is willing, but the flesh is weak." Again he went away for the second time and prayed, "My Father, if this cannot pass unless I drink it, your will be done." Again he came and found them sleeping, for their eyes were heavy. So leaving them again, he went away and prayed for the third time, saying the same words. Then he came to the disciples and said to them, "Are you still sleeping and taking your rest? See, the hour is at hand, and the Son of Man is betrayed into the hands of sinners. Get up, let us be going. See, my betrayer is at hand."

*NRSVCE

The Agony in the Garden
Fruit: Sorrow for Sin

The Sorrowful Mysteries: Prayed Tuesdays and Fridays

The Scourging at the Pillar
Pilate Addresses the Crowd (Luke 23: 13-16)*

Pilate then called together the chief priests, the leaders, and the people, and said to them, "You brought me this man as one who was perverting the people; and here I have examined him in your presence and have not found this man guilty of any of your charges against him. Neither has Herod, for he sent him back to us. Indeed, he has done nothing to deserve death. I will therefore have him flogged and release him."

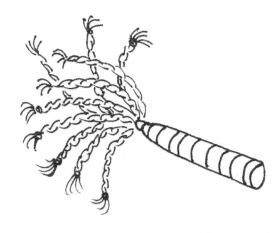

*NRSVCE

The Second Sorrowful Mystery

Scourging at the Pillar
Fruit: Purity

The Sorrowful Mysteries: Prayed Tuesdays and Fridays

The Crowning of Thorns
The Soldiers Mock Jesus (John 19: 2-5)

the soldiers wove a crown of thorns and put it on his head, and they dressed him in a purple robe. 3 They kept coming up to him, saying, "Hail, King of the Jews!" and striking him on the face. 4 Pilate went out again and said to them, "Look, I am bringing him out to you to let you know that I find no case against him." 5 So Jesus came out, wearing the crown of thorns and the purple robe. Pilate said to them, "Here is the man!"

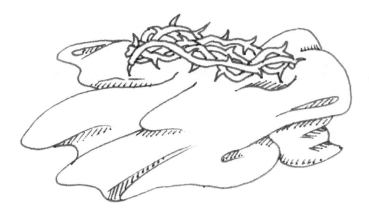

*NRSVCE

The Third Sorrowful Mystery

The Crowning with Thorns
Fruit: Moral Courage

Jesus Carries His Cross
Jesus is Led Off to be Crucified (Luke 23: 26-31)*

As they led him away, they seized a man, Simon of Cyrene, who was coming from the country, and they laid the cross on him, and made him carry it behind Jesus. A great number of the people followed him, and among them were women who were beating their breasts and wailing for him. But Jesus turned to them and said, "Daughters of Jerusalem, do not weep for me, but weep for yourselves and for your children. For the days are surely coming when they will say, 'Blessed are the barren, and the wombs that never bore, and the breasts that never nursed.' Then they will begin to say to the mountains, 'Fall on us'; and to the hills, 'Cover us.' For if they do this when the wood is green, what will happen when it is dry?"

*NRSVCE

The Fourth Sorrowful Mystery

Jesus Carries His Cross
Fruit: Patience

The Crucifixion
Jesus Gives Up His Spirit (John 19: 25-30)*

Standing near the cross of Jesus were his mother, and his mother's sister, Mary the wife of Clopas, and Mary Magdalene. When Jesus saw his mother and the disciple whom he loved standing beside her, he said to his mother, "Woman, here is your son." Then he said to the disciple, "Here is your mother." And from that hour the disciple took her into his own home.

After this, when Jesus knew that all was now finished, he said (in order to fulfill the scripture), "I am thirsty." A jar full of sour wine was standing there. So they put a sponge full of the wine on a branch of hyssop and held it to his mouth. When Jesus had received the wine, he said, "It is finished." Then he bowed his head and gave up his spirit.

*NRSVCE

The Fifth Sorrowful Mystery

The Crucifixion of Jesus
Fruit: Perseverence

The Glorious Mysteries: Prayed Sundays and Wednesdays

The Resurrection
The Empty Tomb (Matthew 28: 1-10)*

After the sabbath, as the first day of the week was dawning, Mary Magdalene and the other Mary went to see the tomb. And suddenly there was a great earthquake; for an angel of the Lord, descending from heaven, came and rolled back the stone and sat on it. His appearance was like lightning, and his clothing white as snow. For fear of him the guards shook and became like dead men. But the angel said to the women, "Do not be afraid; I know that you are looking for Jesus who was crucified. 6 He is not here; for he has been raised, as he said. Come, see the place where he lay. Then go quickly and tell his disciples, 'He has been raised from the dead, and indeed he is going ahead of you to Galilee; there you will see him.' This is my message for you." So they left the tomb quickly with fear and great joy, and ran to tell his disciples. Suddenly Jesus met them and said, "Greetings!" And they came to him, took hold of his feet, and worshiped him. Then Jesus said to them, "Do not be afraid; go and tell my brothers to go to Galilee; there they will see me."

*NRSVCE

The First Glorious Mystery

The Resurrection
Fruit: Faith

The Ascension of Jesus
(Acts 1: 6-11)*

So when they had come together, they asked him, "Lord, is this the time when you will restore the kingdom to Israel?" He replied, "It is not for you to know the times or periods that the Father has set by his own authority. But you will receive power when the Holy Spirit has come upon you; and you will be my witnesses in Jerusalem, in all Judea and Samaria, and to the ends of the earth." When he had said this, as they were watching, he was lifted up, and a cloud took him out of their sight. While he was going and they were gazing up toward heaven, suddenly two men in white robes stood by them. They said, "Men of Galilee, why do you stand looking up toward heaven? This Jesus, who has been taken up from you into heaven, will come in the same way as you saw him go into heaven."

*NRSVCE

The Ascension
Fruit: Hope

The Second Glorious Mystery

The Glorious Mysteries: Prayed Sundays and Wednesdays

The Descent of the Holy Spirit
Pentecost (Acts 2:1-4)

When the day of Pentecost had come, they were all together in one place. And suddenly from heaven there came a sound like the rush of a violent wind, and it filled the entire house where they were sitting. Divided tongues, as of fire, appeared among them, and a tongue rested on each of them. All of them were filled with the Holy Spirit and began to speak in other languages, as the Spirit gave them ability.

Third Glorious Mystery

Descent of the Holy Spirit
Fruit: Love

The Glorious Mysteries: Prayed Sundays and Wednesdays

The The Assumption of Mary
Mary Meets the Lord in the Sky (Luke 1: 46-56)*

And Mary said,

"My soul magnifies the Lord, and my spirit rejoices in God my Savior, for he has looked with favor on the lowliness of his servant.

Surely, from now on all generations will call me blessed; for the Mighty One has done great things for me, and holy is his name.

*NRSVCE

Fourth Glorious Mystery

The Assumption of Mary
Fruit: Grace of a Happy Death

The Glorious Mysteries: Prayed Sundays and Wednesdays

The Crowning of Mary
The Woman and the Dragon (Revelation 12: 1-5)*

A great portent appeared in heaven: a woman clothed with the sun, with the moon under her feet, and on her head a crown of twelve stars. She was pregnant and was crying out in birth pangs, in the agony of giving birth. Then another portent appeared in heaven: a great red dragon, with seven heads and ten horns, and seven diadems on his heads. His tail swept down a third of the stars of heaven and threw them to the earth. Then the dragon stood before the woman who was about to bear a child, so that he might devour her child as soon as it was born. And she gave birth to a son, a male child, who is to rule all the nations with a rod of iron.

*NRSVCE

The Fifth Glorious Mystery

The Crowning of Mary
Fruit: Trust in Mary's Prayers for us

In Closing...

Hail, holy Queen, Mother of mercy,

Our life, our sweetness and our hope,

To thee do we cry, poor banished children of Eve.

To thee do we send up our sighs,

Mourning and weeping in this valley of tears.

Turn then, most gracious advocate,

Your eyes of Mercy towards us,

And after this, our exile, show unto us

The blessed fruit of thy womb, Jesus

O clement, o loving, o sweet Virgin Mary,

Pray for us, O Holy Mother of God,

That we may be made worthy of the

Promises of Christ. Amen

Oh Lord, whose only begotten Son, through his life, death, and resurrection, has purchased for us the rewards of eternal life, grant, we besech Thee, that by meditating upon these mysteries of the Holy Rosary of the Blessed Virgin Mary, we may both imitate what they contain, and obtain what they promise through the same Christ, Our Lord, Amen.

In the name of the Father and the Son and the Holy Spirit, Amen

Made in the USA
Monee, IL
02 December 2020

50456577R00031